THE CHRISTIAN FAITH

Glimpses of Church History

by J.C. WENGER

HERALD PRESS
Scottdale, Pennsylvania
Kitchener, Ontario

THE CHRISTIAN FAITH

Copyright © 1971 by Herald Press, Scottdale, Pa. 15683
Library of Congress Catalog Card Number: 71-153968
International Standard Book Number: 0-8361-1646-1
Printed in the United States of America
Design by Jan Gleysteen

Second Printing, 1976

To the Memory of

JOHN S. COFFMAN
1848 - 1899

Humble Man of God
Earnest Disciple of Christ
Effective Herald of the Gospel

FOREWORD

This unit on church history is but a brief summary statement of a few highlights of the history of Christ's church from Pentecost until the present time. At the most, one may hope that it will create enough interest to move a few persons to begin seriously to read church history. Maybe it can whet a few intellectual appetites!

As a Christian theist, and standing in an evangelical tradition, I make no apology for referring to the bodily resurrection of our Lord, to His having sent the Holy Spirit in new fullness upon His waiting disciples on the day of Pentecost, and to seeing His hand in the renewal of the church and in its missionary outreach.

The story of the rise and spread of the Christian faith is without parallel in human history. No Christian can afford to be ignorant of it. Here we see the mighty hand of God, and the story has not yet ended. It is the command of our risen Lord that we are to make disciples of all the nations. How glorious it is to have even a small part in that great commission!

Associated Mennonite Biblical Seminaries
J. C. Wenger
Elkhart, Indiana
March 10, 1970

CONTENTS

I

Tbe Cburcb Cbrist Founded

The Founder of the Church

Christians recognize Jesus Christ as the founder of the Christian church. Christ was born around 5 B.C. (the monk who computed B.C. and A.D. made a mistake of a few years) in Bethlehem in the land of Palestine. At the age of thirty He emerged from obscurity, having been a house-builder in the town of Nazareth in the district of Galilee. He accepted baptism from a Jewish preacher named John the Baptist. Christ's baptism was a sort of ordination to begin His public ministry of God's Word.

For some three years He went about in the land of Palestine, preaching repentance from sin and a life of faith, holiness, and love. About A.D. 30 He was put to death by crucifixion, with the sentence pronounced by a

Roman procurator, Pontius Pilate. This deed resulted from the moblike insistence of the Jewish hierarchy and its supporters who regarded Christ as a blasphemer because He called Himself the Son of God. Jesus also assumed the lofty Messianic title, "Son of man" (Daniel 7:13). We call the day of the crucifixion, Good Friday, for on that day the incarnate Son of God made atonement for the sins of the world.

On the third day, as the Jews reckoned time, Christ arose from the dead in the body in which He had suffered and showed Himself to His disciples, especially to His twelve apostles whom He had chosen and taught to become the leaders of the church He planned to establish. After forty days of such appearances and teaching, He ascended back to heaven.

Flaming Heralds

When Christ died, the hopes of the apostles died too. They felt that all their hopes for the firm establishment of the kingdom of God had fallen through. But Christ's resurrection changed them from dispirited and broken men to flaming heralds of His deity and lordship.

Before His ascension Christ commissioned His followers to make disciples of all the nations, teaching them all that He had taught the apostles and promising that He Himself would ever be with them. But tarry in Jerusalem, He commanded, until you are endued with power from on high. This they did.

They had only ten days to wait. The day of the great enduement of power came on the Jewish festival day known as Pentecost (held on a Sunday, fifty days after the second day of the Jewish festival known as the Passover). On this particular Pentecost day, now often called Whitsunday, seven weeks after Easter, about the year A.D. 30, those who believed on Christ were all together, possibly in the Jerusalem temple, when there was a great outpouring of the Holy Spirit on the believers. God attested to this birthday of the church by causing "tongues as of fire" to rest upon the heads of the anointed ones, and they were filled with great joy as they proclaimed the mighty works of God.

Visitors from many lands were present, and to their astonishment they heard these believers praising God in their several languages. This "Whitsunday" or Pentecost was the birthday of the Christian church. From this day the apostles and other believers went everywhere telling the "good news" (the gospel) that Christ has taken away the sins of the world, that God accepts as His sons and daughters all those who turn from sin ("repent") and who are ready to make their covenant of discipleship with the Lord Jesus Christ. The sign of this covenant was water baptism, a sign used also by John the Baptist to signify repentance from sin.

On this great day of Pentecost Peter preached a sermon which explained the meaning of the strange events people witnessed and tied the phenomena to Old Testament prophecy (Joel 2 had predicted just such an outpouring of the Holy Spirit). Peter called upon the Jews to repent and unite with the believers on Christ. About three thousand converts responded and were baptized with water. Thus the church began.

Early Progress

As to theology (the system of thinking about man's relationship with God), the greatest problem faced by the early Jewish church was how to relate to the ceremonial law of Moses: holy days, clean and unclean foods, circumcision as a religious rite, and the like. An important conference of the Jerusalem church (Acts 15) with its local leaders called elders, and with the apostles present, took place about twenty years after Pentecost (A.D. 50). After thorough debate and discussion they came unanimously to the conclusion that Gentile believers were basically free from the ceremonial laws of the Old Testament.

Such freedom from legalism is often called Christian freedom. It means that Christianity is not a neo-Judaism, nor any other system of do's and don'ts. Much less is it freedom to live in sin. Christian freedom means rather that Christ by His Spirit delivers from the slavery of sin and also changes the inner nature of the believer so that he hates sin but longs to do the will of his Lord. He wants to please Christ. He is not under law, but above it. He does not have his eye on the law but on his Lord, and as he joyously serves Christ he attains the intent of the law.

The other area of progress was in evangelistic outreach. At first the Jewish believers more or less huddled together in Jerusalem, fearing at times the harsh attempts of the Jewish hierarchy to suppress the new religion by force. In the course of time the early church felt led to choose seven Spirit-filled men to care for the needs of their poor. These seven came eventually to be recognized as the forerunners of such stewards as were given the name of deacons (a Greek word meaning servants, those who minister).

One of the seven was called Stephen, a mighty man in the Scriptures and a powerful witness of the new gospel. Stephen incurred the hostility of the Jewish leaders and was stoned to death for being such an effective witness. The Greek word for witness *marturia* came to mean a martyr, a person who was put to death for giving his witness to Christ. Indeed such a death was often the most effective witness of a person's entire career.

A severe persecution of the early believers broke out in connection with the martyrdom of Stephen, and the Jerusalem believers were widely scattered in Palestine. Wherever they went, they faithfully shared the good news that the crucified, resurrected, and ascended Christ was now both Lord and Savior, able to deliver any sinner from his guilt and bondage if he turns from sin to Christ. There is salvation from sin in Jesus Christ! Thus persecution, although not so intended, led directly to a great increase in the number of believers.

But the greatest outreach of all came through a man named Paul (Saul in Hebrew), of the university town of Tarsus in Asia Minor (now Turkey). After his conversion to Christ, he was brought to the early group of believers at Antioch in Syria, a town along the eastern end of the Mediterranean Sea, north of Palestine. There he was one of the leaders in the study of God's Word (the Jewish Scriptures, commonly called the Old Testament now).

After much Bible study and prayer, the Holy Spirit put into the hearts of the Antioch believers (here called Christians for the first time) to send out two missionaries into the Graeco-Roman world. The two chosen were Barnabas and Saul (Paul). During the 40's and 50's Paul and his colleagues conducted three great missionary campaigns, usually several years in length, and extending across Asia Minor to cities like Ephesus, and even into Greece (Athens and Corinth). Everywhere Paul went, he began his gospel ministry in the synagogues where he won many Jews. There were also many Gentiles in those days who, although often not bothering to become full Jews by circumcision, worshiped the God of Israel, the Lord God.

Multitudes of these so-called "Proselytes of the Gate" (they had not fully entered the Jewish fold) also responded to Paul's evangelistic efforts, which extended all the way to Rome, and thus the church of the early Roman Empire, although born in Judaism, soon had a strong Gentile complexion. It was this problem (whether Gentile Christians also needed to become Jews by circumcision and the observance of the ceremonial law of Moses) which precipitated the great Jerusalem council of A.D. 50 referred to earlier.

As we noted then, the discussions at Jerusalem were a glorious victory for Christian freedom. (The Jewish Christians who were unable to see the truth of Christian freedom were called Judaizers. Paul's letter called Galatians is a direct answer to the error of the Judaizers.)

The Faith of the Early Church

The Christian of the 40's and 50's accepted the Jewish Bible as his very own. He put his faith in the Lord God just as did his Jewish neighbors. But in addition, he was deeply conscious of being a believer on the Messiah ("Christ" in Greek) to whom the Scriptures of the Old Testament pointed. He believed that this Messiah had come in the person of Jesus of Nazareth, commonly called Jesus, Christ, or Jesus the Christ.

Indeed Christ soon became a second name, so that in the writings of the New Testament the Messiah was often called Jesus Christ, or even Christ Jesus. The early Christians read the Old Testament Messianically (Christologically). That is, they saw Jesus as the One who had fulfilled the Messianic prophecies of the Old Testament. But even more, they saw Christ mirrored in many passages which had until then not been considered to refer directly to the Messiah. The New Testament writings quote or allude to Old Testament passages over 2,000 times.

In common with the Jews the early Christians believed in God both as the creator and as a God of providence. They believed that God hears and answers prayer. They believed that the Scriptures were the holy oracles of God. They believed in a life of holiness and love. They believed in a future resurrection and judgment, and in the afterlife. (The Jewish party known as the Sadducees denied the resurrection, however.) They believed in the importance of corporate worship services.

The early Christians broke with the Jews by holding that Jesus was in very truth the Messiah who was to come and that He had fulfilled the Messianic prophecies. It all came to pass in His life just as it was written in the prophets! This Jesus was God's revelatory Word to mankind, the disclosure of all that God is.

Jesus was a *prophet* in that He made known by His words and in His very person who God was and what He is like. Jesus was a *priest* in that by offering Himself on the cross of Golgotha He had died in our stead, made atonement for our sins, conquered the forces of sin and death, and reconciled us to God the Father. He has now ascended to the right hand of God (the place of supreme authority) in the heavens. He has sent the Holy Spirit to convict men of their need of a Savior and to sanctify and lead all Christian believers. As *king*, Jesus Christ is our Lord (the earliest and simplest Christian confession of faith declared simply: JESUS IS LORD), and we are the happy subjects in His kingdom.

As our Lord and Savior, Jesus Christ will return on the Great Day to raise the dead and judge the world and to take His own into the glories of the eternal kingdom. Meanwhile Christians want to make as many disciples for Him as they possibly can. There was therefore a great note of victory in the church when

Paul and his helpers reported back to the church in Antioch how God had blessed their missionary efforts in the conversion of many people to faith in Christ.

The Book of Acts, by Luke the physician, who was also a traveling companion of the Apostle Paul, seems to take special delight in emphasizing how successful the evangelistic and missionary witness of the early church was. First there were 120 believers, then accessions of three thousand, then the believers number five thousand, and after a time tens of thousands ("myriads") are believers (See Acts 1:15; 2:41; 4:4; 21:20). Luke continually stressed how the Word of God kept growing (that is, it was ever more widely proclaimed), and the number of disciples kept increasing daily (Acts 6:7; 12:24; 16:5; 19:20).

The Life of the Early Church

The best source on the life of the early church is the Book of Acts to which reference has just been made. We can read "between the lines" of Paul's letters as to some of the problems which the early church had to face and on which Paul gave his fatherly counsel.

Perhaps the very best description of the life of the Apostolic Church is found in Acts 2:42. There we learn that the early Christians "continued steadfastly" in four things: (1) in the *teaching* of the apostles: which means the truth about Jesus Christ who died for our sins and rose again for our justification, who is at the right hand of God, and who will one day come for us; (2) in Christian *fellowship*, that is, they cultivated the fellowship of the Spirit, maintaining open communication with each other, rejoicing in the brotherhood of love and goodwill of which each was a full member, and avoiding any quarrels or grudges which would mar the joy of that holy fellowship; (3) in the *breaking of bread*, that is, they met together frequently to eat the Lord's Supper together, a joyful commemoration, using bread and wine to call to remembrance the way Christ suffered His body to be broken, and His blood to be shed in our behalf: this communion meal was often called the Eucharist in the early centuries of the church — the meal of thanks-giving; and (4) in the *prayers* (thus the Greek), that is, the Christian believers — then still Jewish by race — met together at stated times for common prayer.

So great was their sense of love and unity that they gave up holding private property for a time, simply sharing with one another as each one had need (Acts 2:44). As loyal Jews they continued to share in the daily temple worship (Acts 2:46), but they also met together as Christians in private homes to "remember the Lord" in their Eucharist-meal, the Lord's Supper (Acts 2:46). Perhaps the most dominant note of their lives was Christian joy — they had "gladness and singleness of heart," and they were continually praising God (Acts 2:46, 47).

Simple Organization

The early church had no complicated organizational pattern. Soon local congregations of believers developed, especially when the church was established in various towns and cities across Asia Minor and Greece. The early Christian assemblies, being Jewish at first, took over the synagogue pattern, which was to choose several elders in each congregation, men who were in a general way the leaders of the congregation.

The Greek word for elder is *presbyter*, from which the Presbyterian Church takes its name. These elders assumed the general oversight of the congregations or assemblies (in Greek, *ecclesia* means assembly), and they were therefore also called overseers (the Greek word is *episkopos*, now generally translated bishop, and it literally means one having oversight). Soon it was decided to set aside certain brothers to assist in the work of the church, and they came to be known as *deacons*, that is, those rendering service.

At first there were no area overseers for the local elder-bishops and deacons. The overseer of the elders and the church was

Christ through His Spirit. There were also no area conferences or synods, for why would the church need them? Neither were there general synods or conferences. The key concept was simplicity, copied from the Jewish synagogue system, which arose during the exile of the Jews prior to the time of Christ.

There were also no mission boards, for every Christian was a witness. There were no church buildings, for the temple of the Jews was still open to the new believers on Christ. Smaller groups met locally in private homes. We therefore often read of "house" congregations in the New Testament: one met in the house of Aquila and Priscilla (Romans 16:3-5; 1 Corinthians 16:19), another in the house of Nymphas (Colossians 4:15). The era of chapel and cathedral building was yet in the distant future.

The church was the new people of God, united through its common faith in Christ and created and maintained by the Holy Spirit. It was a church ready to bear the cross— the price of Christian discipleship in a society which was not yet ready for the concept of open-minded toleration. It was a church which looked forward with eager joy for the return of its risen Lord. This church which was much concerned for the whole man put great emphasis on evangelism, nurture, and service. It was a happy church.

Quesions for Review,
Thought, and Further Reading

1. Who founded the Christian church, and how did He do it?
2. How does the Lord use His church to add members to the body of Christ?
3. Who was the great missionary of the early church? Who commissioned him?
4. What was the initial difference between a Jewish believer and a Christian believer?
5. What fourfold description of Christian perseverance is given of the early church?
6. How can the church maintain Christian simplicity while organizing to meet the challenges of today's world?
7. Should people with an assignment (minister or deacon) think of the power they have, or should they think of themselves as love-servants of Christ's body?
8. How can a local congregation share in the greater wisdom of the larger brotherhood without beclouding the primary authority of the local assembly?
9. Have you additional questions to present to a minister of the gospel or other believer as to the early church?
10. Why do you think the early Christians were happy even in days of persecution?

2

NUMERICAL GROWTH AND SPIRITUAL DECLINE

The Great Work of the Apostle Paul

The Apostle Paul undertook three massive evangelistic campaigns across Asia Minor, reaching even to Athens and Corinth in Greece. His first campaign (Acts 13, 14) was in the late 40's. The great question of Christian freedom was settled at the Jerusalem council of A.D. 50. This was followed by the second campaign (Acts 15:36 — 18:22), of about A.D. 51-53.

On the second campaign or "journey" Paul wrote his first two letters to the Thessalonians about A.D. 52, setting forth the Christian hope of Christ's return and its significance for both Christians and unbelievers. The third campaign (Acts 18:23 — 20:3) lasted from about A.D. 54 to 58. During that span Paul wrote four more of his great "epistles" (letters) to the churches: Galatians, about A.D. 55; 1 and 2 Corinthians, about A.D. 57, and Romans about A.D. 58.

When Paul returned to Jerusalem, he underwent arrest (Acts 22:25), brought about by the hostility of the anti-Christian Jews, A.D. 58, and he sat in prison in Caesarea for two years (A.D. 58-60). This story is told in Acts 23 — 26. The last two chapters of Acts (27, 28) recount Paul's experiences on the way to Rome as a prisoner who had appealed to the higher court of the emperor and his dwelling two years under house arrest in Rome (A.D. 61-63).

During this Roman imprisonment Paul wrote his four great prison epistles: Colossians, Philemon, Ephesians, and Philippians. After this period, Paul seems to have been released for another stint of missionary service, only to be arrested and imprisoned a second time (possibly A.D. 65-67), after which he suffered martyrdom under the Emperor Nero about A.D. 67. During this second Roman imprisonment he may have written the so-called pastoral epistles: 1 Timothy, Titus, and 2 Timothy.

Paul was the greatest missionary of all time. He could enter a pagan city, find the synagogue, preach to the Jews and Proselytes of the Gate there, win a goodly number of converts, organize them into a congregation, supervise the election of elders, and then move on to another city. He was a man of a deeply emotional nature, a man who shed tears of concern for the welfare of people and churches, a man who constantly agonized in intercessory prayer for the spiritual welfare of the young assemblies of believers. He was also a man of mighty intellect as even a cursory reading of his letters reveals.

God prepared a Paul, with his large heart, his strong will, and his powerful mind, called him into His kingdom, and anointed him with Holy Spirit fullness. Thus God had a servant whom. He could use in a remarkable way for the establishment of a chain of congregations from Jerusalem to Rome. Paul thought through the issues of the Christian faith in a fruitful manner as he wrote almost half of the books of the New Testament!

At the center of Paul's life and thought stood his Lord, Jesus Christ, the crucified and risen Messiah. Paul saw converts to the faith being introduced to and "identified" with Christ in heart, will, and evangelistic intention.

Just as Christ died and rose again, so do converts to Christ die to sin and rise to a new life. Such believers are spiritually so united to Christ by the Holy Spirit that they may be described as being "in Christ" — a concept found about 164 times in Paul and about 200 times in the entire New Testament. Paul gloried in "salvation by grace through faith," and in God's way of providing the righteousness which He demands: a righteousness through faith in Christ (Romans 1:17; 3:21-31). He was also the irrefutable champion of Christian freedom from any and all legalisms.

Other Early Leaders

The twelve apostles, except for Judas, also labored strenuously and faithfully for the extension of the kingdom of Christ. No wholly reliable records remain as to their several places of labor, but the traditions of the church report the supposed end of each. The New Testament reports the death of James, the brother of John, by beheading (Acts 12:2) about A.D. 44. Tradition says that Philip was stoned to death at Hierapolis in Phrygia A.D. 54. James, the brother of our Lord, is said to have been cast down from the temple, then clubbed to death, A.D. 62.

Peter is said to have been crucified at Rome under Nero in the late 60's insisting on being crucified head downward, for he was not worthy to hang like his Lord. Andrew is said to have been crucified in Achaia about A.D. 70. Bartholomew is said to have gone to Armenia, where he was flayed and beheaded about A.D. 70. Thomas is said to have gone to India, and perished in the Far East by torture and being speared. Only John died a natural death in the late 90's after surviving extreme torture which included being thrown into hot oil!

James, the Lord's brother, who is reported to have been clubbed to death, has the distinction of having written the earliest New Testament book, the Epistle of James, somewhere around A.D. 45. He does not even use the later common designation of *ecclesia* for the local Christian assembly, but calls it a *synagogue* (another Greek word for assembly). James 2:2. He seems to have served as a kind of moderator of the Jerusalem church from the 40's until his death about A.D. 62.

Other early leaders were Timothy, the young colleague of Paul, and one Simeon, who succeeded James the Lord's brother. Simeon is said to have been a blood relative of Christ and was the son of a man named Clopas. He was crucified at an advanced age in A.D. 107. He is not mentioned in the New Testament, for the chief history of the early church, Acts, closes with Paul's first Roman imprisonment about A.D. 63.

Other Ancient Leaders

After the days of the apostles (from about A.D. 90 through the second century) God raised up other leaders who blessed the church by their ministry of the Word, including their writings. Mention must be made of Clement of Rome, Hermas, Ignatius of Antioch, Polycarp, Papias, Barnabas, the unknown author of the *Didache* — the *Teaching* of the twelve apostles, Montanus, Tertullian, and Irenaeus. After the second century came Clement of Alexandria (died about 220), Origen (died about 254), Cyprian (d. 258), Eusebius (d. 340), Athanasius (d. 373), Jerome (d. 420), and the greatest of them all, Augustine (d. 430). The great scholar of the Middle Ages was Thomas Aquinas (d. 1274), whose basic teachings are still largely normative for Roman Catholicism.

Church Centers

It has been pointed out that in a very real sense the spiritual center of the church from its inception in A.D. 30 until about A.D. 45 was Jerusalem, with men like Peter and John serving as the most significant leaders while the church was almost purely Jewish. About A.D. 45, when the missionary-minded Antioch church assumed responsibility for sending out missionaries into the Graeco-Roman world, Antioch in Syria became the spiritual center of the new strongly Gentile church.

Paul's leadership probably lasted until the mid 60's when the Apostle John had his working base on the west coast of Asia Minor. The center of the church shifted from the mid 60's to the late 90's to the great city Ephesus. Thus the center of the church tended to move westward during the first century. Unfortunately, the Jews of Palestine revolted against Rome in A.D. 66, and Jerusalem finally fell to the Roman general Titus who wreaked unbelievable vengeance on the defeated city, completely destroying it, A.D. 70.

Still more unfortunately, the Jewish Christians tended to break up into various sects, many of whom were not wholly sound in the faith. From the late first century to the present time, the church has been a strongly Gentile body ethnically.

Enormous Outreach

If the early historians of the church knew anything of their subject, the church spread out into the civilized Graeco-Roman world with remarkable speed. Historical research and archaeological evidence lend support to the widespread distribution of the Christian church of the first centuries. By A.D. 180 Christianity had surrounded the great Mediterranean Sea — which is 2,000 miles long. At the Council of Arles in France, A.D. 314, bishops were present from France, Germany, and England. This was only 284 years after the day of Pentecost — a truly remarkable growth.

In many cases the prominent name now associated with the conversion of a people may be that of a man well remembered, though not necessarily the first missionary to that area. In Ireland, for example, the well-remembered man was the famous Patrick, who early in the fifth century served as a slave in Ireland, and who later (431) returned to evangelize the island with great success.

At that point there had likely been Christians in Ireland for 200 years. Likewise the six waves of Germanic peoples who came to England, 449-547, called for fresh evangelistic and missionary endeavor. The great missionary among the German Goths was Ulfilas of the fourth century, who translated the Bible into Gothic.

In the early centuries of the Christian era there were a few Christians in Switzerland, but much of that land was overrun by the Germanic people, the Alamanni, beginning perhaps as early as the fourth century, but for the most part after 400. Columbanus, an Irish monk, established mission work among the Swiss Alamanni about two centuries later (early seventh century), but was soon forced to relocate in North Italy.

The rather uncultured Germanic peoples were slowly evangelized from the fourth to the ninth centuries, the Scandinavians in the tenth, and finally the Russians in the late tenth century. (The gospel was preached in Russia as early as the ninth century, but Christianity did not become the official faith of the country until A.D. 988.)

Losses to Islam

The staunchly monotheistic Mohammedan faith (Islam) was founded by the prophet Mohammed (c. 570-629), an Arab who was familiar with the Jewish and Christian Scriptures, in the early seventh century. The Arabs did not hesitate to use the sword to make converts, and in a manner **deeply** alarming to Christians Islam spread across North Africa and crossed over into Spain. It must be admitted that Christianity at this time was in spiritual decline. Islam spread around the eastern end of the Mediterranean Sea, and westward through the Balkan states, largely wiping out Christianity as it went.

This huge pincer movement left a non-Christian band around the Mediterranean, with Christian Europe shaking in its shoes in the sixteenth century. (The Mohammedans were stopped in Spain in 732, but even as late as 1453 Constantinople fell to them.) In the eleventh, twelfth, and thirteenth centuries the European Christians made many "crusades" trying to capture the Holy Land from the Arabs.

Persecution of Christians

As early as the 40's the Jewish authorities in Jerusalem instituted repressive measures against Christians. In the year A.D. 64 the Emperor Nero, after perhaps setting fire to

nature took place. Creedalism, in some respects, became a substitute for genuine discipleship. The sacraments came to be thought of as the major channels of grace. The ministers of the Word became "priests," with a much higher status than the ordinary people, the "laity." The mass came ultimately to be regarded as a meritorious (although bloodless) repetition of Christ's sacrifice on the cross. Prayer was offered to Mary, to various apostles and deceased "saints," and to angels.

A doctrine of purgatory (a place of temporary punishment) developed. And the church finally believed that it was the custodian of the "Treasury of Merits" — excess merits with God earned by Christ and various outstanding saints, and which Treasury the church could tap for the benefit of those earning an "indulgence," that is, a cancellation of more or less of what was scheduled for one in purgatory.

The Bible retreated more and more into the background, as this sacramentalism and hierarchical structure came to the fore. The papacy was finally a worldly office, with popes struggling with kings for supremacy, and using the same tactics as the kings — intrigue, bribery, war, and the like. There was immorality in high places in the church.

From 600 to 1500 the church was in a state of grave spiritual need — although it grew rich in wealth and possessions. Monasticism was a reaction and a counterweight to the secularization of the church. Monks and nuns lived apart from the world, and spent much time in meditation and prayer. The monasteries also did much to keep learning alive during the "Dark Ages."

Serious men of God pondered the question, Will the church ever again be the holy institution of God which it was when it had no power or prestige in the days of the apostles, but when it was a holy community of earnest disciples of the Lord Jesus, ready to bear the cost of discipleship, of Christian cross-bearing?

Questions for Review, Thought, and Further Reading

1. What characteristics in Paul made him an effective missionary?
2. In what sense are Christians "united to" or "in" Christ? In what sense is there a total difference between the Christian and his Lord?
3. How do you account for the hatred of the ancient world against the Christians who went everywhere with the good news of salvation, and living by love?

4. Describe the three centers of the early church. In what direction was the movement?

5. Did Christians do right or wrong when they fought with the Mohammedans? If wrong, what should they have done?

6. What was the Constantinian synthesis? Why may this have been a "fall" for the church?

7. Can you find out more about the crusades? What do you think of the project in general? of the children's crusade?

8. Describe the outward developments and the inner decline of the ancient church.

9. Did monasticism rest on Christian assumptions? If so, what were they? What particular achievement do the monks get credit for?

10. Do you suppose that there were many individual Christians of prayer and obedience during the long centuries when the church was seriously corrupt?

3

GOD SENDS REFORMERS TO THE MEDIEVAL CHURCH

Peter Waldo

As the church sank lower and lower in its spiritual level, God raised up men of the Word to try to lead His wayward people back to a more biblical doctrine and life. Undoubtedly, even the names and memories of some of these conscientious and brave men of God are lost. And there will be space in this chapter for only four representative pre-sixteenth-century reformers.

The first is Peter Waldo of France. The exact year of his birth is not known, but since he was a wealthy merchant by the 1170's, and since he died about 1217, it is thought that he was born about 1140. In the 1170's he was living at Lyons in Southern France. He had also become a devoted student of the New Testament — and also saw to it that manuscript copies of a French vernacular version of the New Testament were made from the Latin.

Waldo must have made a special study of Christ's Sermon on the Mount (Matthew 5 — 7), for he stressed a life of simplicity, the renunciation of wealth-seeking, any taking of human life as in war and in capital punishment, the rejection of the oath, disbelief in purgatory, the shunning of worldly theaters and dances, staying away from taverns, and the like. He and his followers, often called "Poor Men of Lyons," were bitterly critical of the Roman Catholic Church, and of those clergy whose lives they considered unworthy. Waldo's followers, known as Waldenses, rejected the dedication of church buildings and the worship of "relics" (supposedly sacred objects associated with Christ, with His apostles, or with various martyrs).

After making provision for his wife and children he gave away the rest of the riches he had accumulated as a merchant, and devoted himself to the teaching of the gospel. He and his followers went about in simple clothing, wearing sandals or going barefoot, and living from whatever people gave them.

The pope was of course unhappy with Waldo's radical critique of the Roman Church, and in 1179 ordered him to quit preaching. Feeling that he ought to obey God rather than men, Waldo paid no attention to the order. In 1184 Pope Lucius III excommunicated him — which did not bother him. He went right on living as he understood the New Testament to teach disciples of Christ to live.

Many Waldenses committed vast portions of Scripture to memory. (From living in the Alpine mountain valleys of the Piedmont in Northern Italy, the Waldenses were often also called *Vaudois,* a word which may mean the valley people.)

The Waldensian movement spread rapidly. They had their own bishops, ministers, and deacons. Eventually, there were Waldenses scattered widely in Europe — France, Italy, Germany, and Spain. Waldo himself is said to have died in Bohemia about 1217. His followers were hardly prepared for the savage persecution which often came upon them. The Dominican inquisition was especially difficult. In the course of time they lost their doctrine of nonresistance, perhaps through the loss of many leaders in persecution.

In 1487 Pope Innocent VIII ordered their total extermination, but the project did not fully succeed. By the 1530's they were receiving baptism and communion from Roman priests, yet they maintained their own identity and preserved their unique disciplinary standards. They wrote to the Swiss Reformed leader,

Oecolampad, seeking his counsel and guidance on various points. He ordered them to make a total break with Rome, which they did, and since that time they are reckoned as a part of the Protestant Reformation. They finally achieved full religious liberty in 1848.

In 1823 a British clergyman named W. S. Gilly visited them, and wrote a book entitled, *A Visit to the Valleys of the Piedmont*. This book fell into the hands of a British colonel, J. C. Beckwith (1789-1862), who had lost a leg in the Battle of Waterloo in 1815, and he saw in the need of the Waldenses a cause which could give meaning to his life. For thirty-five years Beckwith lived among them, helping them build a church building in Turin, and establishing 120 schools for their children.

The Waldenses also established a theological school to train their ministers. At first it was located at one of their centers, Torre Pellice, near Turin, but in 1861 it was relocated at Florence; since 1920 it is in Rome. The Waldenses now number about 20,000. In many respects they are entitled to the label, "The oldest Protestant Church in the World."

John Wyclif

A little over a century after Waldo died, a child was born in England who was destined to become a mighty force in the history of the church. Indeed he has been honored with the title, "The Morning Star of the Reformation." Born in the 1320's he became associated with Oxford University. While still in his early 30's he served as Master of Balliol College. He does not seem to have completed his doctorate in theology until the year 1372, according to the *Encyclopaedia Britannica.* As a university professor his lectures were held in high regard by the students.

In the course of time, the whole Christian world knew of the man, his theology, and his gifts. By the 1370's, when he was probably in his 50's, Wyclif was beginning to come to the radical positions which attracted wide attention in the world of his day. He came to believe that the church had no right to be concerned with temporal matters, and clergy should not, he thought, own any property at all.

Wyclif was especially critical of the papacy and of its claims. He ultimately came to the conclusion that the papacy as such could be properly described by the word "Antichrist." This of course did not add to his stature as far as the pope was concerned. But Wyclif marched straight ahead, crying out against all sorts of corruptions in the church, and testing even the time-hallowed doctrines of the church by the Holy Scriptures. He did not deny the presence of Christ in the sacrament of the altar (the bread of the Lord's Supper), but he powerfully objected to the doctrine that the bread literally becomes Christ (transubstantiation). Wyclif held to what he called the "sufficiency of Holy Scripture."

But Wyclif did more than write Latin essays on the corruptions and errors of the Roman Church. He commissioned lay preachers to spread out over England, two by two, to teach the common people what it means to be a Christian. These teachers were known as "Poor Preachers." Wyclif's followers were called *Lollards*, but the exact meaning of the word is not clear. (It was in use as early as 1382.)

Wyclif's preachers opposed the papacy, re-jected requiring the clergy to be celebate, indulgences, the making of religious pilgrimages to "holy sites," and almost everything distinctively Catholic — all on the foundation of following God's Word alone — not tradition. Wyclif is said to have been deeply influenced by the great North African bishop, Aurelius Augustine (354-430).

Perhaps the greatest single achievement of Wyclif was to take the lead in translating the Latin Vulgate into the English of his day and area: the New Testament by around 1380, and the Old Testament a few years later; his chief helper being Nicholas de Hereford. John Purvey revised the whole version by around 1388, greatly improving it. Wyclif suffered a stroke about 1382, and another on December 28, 1384, from which he died three days later on New Year's Eve.

The Catholic Council of Constance in 1415 detailed 267 alleged errors in the teaching of Wyclif, and ordered his bones to be dug up and burned as a heretic — which was duly done by order of one of the popes in 1528.

John Hus

The greatest patriot and reformer of ancient Bohemia, now a part of Czechoslovakia, was the great man of God, John Hus, a fiery disciple of John Wyclif. Born of Czech parents, his name was Jan, and the last name Hus comes from his native village of Husinec in Bohemia. His father died when he was quite young, yet with his mother's encouragement, he labored to secure a good education at the University of Prague, one of the best schools of higher learning in Europe.

Hus was born around A.D. 1371. By 1396 he had earned his Master's degree, and in 1400 he was ordained as a priest. In 1401 he became a dean in the university, and in 1402 its rector. An earnest disciple of Wyclif, though more restrained and conservative, Hus began to have an ever greater influence in the city, especially after becoming preacher in an important chapel named the "Holy Innocents of Bethlehem."

With great moral earnestness, backed up by his own life of purity, Hus began to attack the morals of the clergy, all the way up to the popes. He seemed to fear neither bishops nor kings. He regarded Christ as the head of the church rather than the Roman pontiff. With great courage he took his stand on the Word of God, the Bible, and on that authority he tested the life and doctrine of the clergy, of kings, and of all men. On this ground he dared to assert that many of the popes had been heretics — a daring pronouncement indeed. Even the queen came to hear his sermons. Hus devoured Wyclif's writings.

But the pope was not minded to listen to such charges. John XXIII dealt decisively with the heretic-scholar by solemnly excommunicating him from the communion of the Holy Roman Church (1410). Two years later he put the city of Prague under an *interdict* — an extreme measure which stopped the administration of the sacraments until lifted. To help ease the situation, Hus left the city.

In 1415 Hus was ordered to stand trial at the great Council of Constance, a massive gathering of church leaders to deal with the problem that there were three rival popes in the church at that time, each with some support. (John XXIII was deposed because of various improper deeds and his immoral life, Gregory XII resigned, and Benedict XIII was also deposed.) Hus was given a "safe-conduct," guaranteeing that he would be allowed to return home safely, regardless of the outcome of the trial. King Wenceslaus and Emperor Sigismund issued this *safe-conduct*.

At Constance, Hus was imprisoned. When he was brought to trial before the Council, he had supposed that he would get a respectful hearing. But he was heckled and jeered with loud cries from all directions, so that it was impossible for him to make a reasonable defense. He finally quit trying. He was then told that by falling silent, he was admitting his errors!

Luther knew the events well, and described them thus: "All worked themselves into a rage like wild boars; the bristles of their backs stood on end; they knit their brows and gnashed their teeth against John Hus." After the Council quieted down, Hus cried out in his ringing voice: "I had supposed that there would have been more fairness, kindness, and order in the Council." This deeply impressed the more moderate and humane people there.

On the morning of the second day of Hus's trial (June 7, 1415) Constance grew dark from an eclipse of the sun, so that lights had to be lit in the Council hall, making the occasion all the more impressive. The emperor begged Hus to recant and to throw himself on the grace of the Council, but Hus was a man of conscience who despised trying to save his life by compromising the truth.

In one of his letters Hus wrote this prayer: "O holy Christ! Draw us after Thee. We are weak. . . . Give us a strong and willing spirit. . . . For without Thee we can do nothing. . . . Grant a willing spirit, a fearless heart, true faith, steadfast hope, perfect love, that for Thy sake we may, with patience and joy, surrender our life. Amen."

On the day of his burning, Saturday, July 6, 1415, a paper cap was put on his head with the notation, "This is the arch-heretic," and a bishop intoned, "We commit thy soul to the devil." Hus replied simply, "And I commit it to my most gracious Lord Jesus Christ." Hus declared, "I call God to witness that I have neither taught nor preached what has been falsely laid to my charge, but that the end of all my preaching and writings was to induce my fellowmen to forsake sin. . . ." A German writer said of Hus, *"Im Erliegen siegen, das war sein Los"* (In being overcome, to conquer — that was his lot).

Out of the Hussite movement ultimately came the *Unitas fratrum*, a Czech church of the Word, which played a role in the formation of the Moravian Church. And the father of this fifteenth-century reformation was surely a man of sterling Christian character, a man who loved the Lord and His people, a university rector, one of the greatest preachers of church history.

Girolamo Savonarola

This Italian reformer was born at Ferrara in 1452. He had an unhappy courtship which deeply wounded him, and he removed to the city of Bologna and joined the Dominican Order (1474). In the monastery he was a sort of Italian Luther, fasting and praying with deep fervency, and suffering anguish at the need of reform in the church.

In 1482 he began to preach in the great city of Florence, vigorously denouncing sin and immorality wherever found — even in the clergy. It took almost ten years to get the ear of the city, but he succeeded. He preached like an Old Testament prophet, crying out against the sins of society, sins which called for divine judgment — and which he sincerely believed was about to fall upon the city.

Such throngs came to hear him preach that he had to begin using the cathedral to accommodate the crowds. He was appointed to head the Dominicans in his province, and instituted a stricter rule in the monastery. When a French king occupied the city of Florence, Savonarola won his respect and even seems to have had a hand in getting him to leave. The people almost lionized him as a hero. He is said to have become the most influential man in Florence.

During Lent, 1495, Savonarola reached a new high in revivalistic preaching. He called upon all men, high and low, to turn from sin and live a holy life. And the Florentines responded. Women began to wear plain dresses, bankers and businessmen made restitution for financial wrongdoing, many people gave alms to the poor, and the crowds flocked to the cathedral to hear the earnest sermons of this intense man of God. At home, people who had Bibles began to read them.

In 1497 Savonarola got the people to burn their "vanities" — masquerade masks, indecent books and pictures, and other carnival frivolities — to the singing of hymns! Savonarola was not inclined to spare anyone, and the pope was certain that Savonarola sometimes meant him when he was preaching against sin. Furthermore, Savonarola lent his support to the Florentine democracy — which was allied to France, and therefore hostile to the pontiff. In May 1497, the pope excommunicated the flaming revivalist.

As late as Lent, 1498, Savonarola was able to muster another bonfire for the sinful objects of the Florentines, but this was the last time. The preacher had offended too many weighty citizens, and popular sentiment began to turn against him. His enemies were able to effect his arrest. He was tortured, as was the lot of supposed "heretics" in those days, and the papal commissioners who presided at his trial knew well enough what the pope wanted. They obliged him by putting Savonarola to death by hanging on May 23, 1498, and burning the body to ashes. Yet on the anniversaries of his martyrdom, those who remembered his earnest revivalistic **preaching** placed flowers on the spot of his execution.

The outlook of Savonarola was not altogether that of a pre-sixteenth-century Protestant. In many respects he did not challenge the unbiblical tradition of the church as did Waldo, Wyclif, and Hus. Yet he was an earnest man of God who sought to bring his fellow Italians to a life of humility, holiness, and faithfulness as he understood it.

As a prophet, however, he was not too successful. It was his conviction that he would one day suffer a violent death, but he confidently believed that after his death the church would be renewed, those in unbelief would be converted, and God's Word would be triumphant on the earth. The fact is that no permanent reformation resulted from his sincere and dedicated efforts. Italy remained largely Catholic even after the sixteenth-century Reformation, and even now the Italian church stands in need of revival and renewal.

Questions for Review, Thought, and Further Reading

1. Did Peter Waldo go "too far" in following what he thought the New Testament taught?
2. Does the witness of the Waldenses seem to you to be basically wholesome?
3. Why did the early reformers like Waldo and Wyclif put so much emphasis on the Bible and its sole authority?
4. Who made the first complete English manuscript Bible?
5. In what sense was the burning of Hus illegal, even for a church and state which reserved the right to destroy heretics?
6. How did Savonarola differ from Wyclif, Hus, and Waldo?
7. Where do you think the greatest return to the authority of God's Word is taking place today?
8. Do you want to be a member of a church which takes a stand for strict obedience to the Scriptures?
9. What was the disadvantage of living before printing was invented (about 1450)?

4

SiXTEENTH - CENTURY
REFORM MOVEMENTS

Luther

If there was ever truth in the adage that
an institution is but the lengthened shadow
of a man, the case of Martin Luther is a case
in point. No man ever changed the course of
the church as drastically as the reformer of
Wittenberg. He was born in 1483 at Eisleben
in the "county" of Mansfeld, just across the
line from Electoral Saxony, North Germany.

Luther grew up in the village of Mansfeld
where he attended Latin school. Later (1497)
he went to Magdeburg and attended a school
operated by the Brethren of the Common Life.
Later he studied also at Eisenach, and in 1501
enrolled in the University of Erfurt. There he
earned the BA degree in 1502, and the MA
in 1505. That same year he suddenly decided
to become a monk, and entered the Augustinian

monastery at Erfurt. He was ordained as Roman Catholic priest the spring (April) of 1507. He later (1512) earned his Doctor of Theology degree at the University of Wittenberg, and almost immediately (1513) became the successor of his beloved teacher, John Staupitz.

Up to this time Luther had not seriously questioned the integrity and spiritual trustworthiness of Roman Catholicism. He was, however, disturbed by the corruption in Rome which he visited in 1510. Now Luther had a real problem. Somehow, although he denied himself of much that would have been a pleasure to him — family, personal freedom, wealth — and although he fasted and prayed with great earnestness and regularity, he simply could not find the peace and joy which he craved. He wanted desperately to find for himself the grace of God, and somehow his sacramental and ascetic approach did not lead him to grace. Luther was in deep distress. He sometimes wondered whether he might be doomed to be lost. He could not find a God of grace. No amount of good works, not even severe self-denial, could bring him peace of soul.

And then the light broke through. It happened in a tower of the Black Monastery in Wittenberg. Luther was studying the meaning of Romans 1:17 ("the righteousness of God" — "He who is righteous by faith shall live").

The year was approximately 1514. Up to the moment of this Great Illumination Luther had taken the righteousness of God to mean that quality in the holy God which makes Him hate sin and punish sinners.

Now as he meditated on the revelation of the righteousness of God in the gospel, it suddenly dawned upon Luther that Paul was talking about a *gift* which we receive when we accept the gospel. "A GIFT!" Imagine that! God gives to me, miserable sinner that I am by nature, the GIFT of DIVINE RIGHTEOUSNESS! It flowed through the mind and soul of Luther like a healing balm. He reported later that he felt as if he had been reborn, and had entered into Paradise. He declared that this passage in Paul became for him "the very gate to Paradise." His mind then roamed through Scripture, seizing other similar phrases, "the work of God," which He effects in us; "the wisdom of God," which He grants to us; and the like. Also, " . . . There suddenly came into my mind the thought that if . . . the righteousness of faith is to be for salvation to everyone who believes, then it is not our merit, but the mercy of God." He testified, "Through this word the Holy Spirit enlightened me in the tower."

Luther was now for the first time a really happy and joyous Christian. He was no longer struggling to become "good enough" to be saved. He was now able to rely wholly on Christ for his salvation. It was all a matter of grace. In our relation to God salvation was actually "by grace alone," as Luther would have said it. On our part, it was, said Luther, "by faith alone." In Latin, *sola gratia* (solely grace) and *sola fidei* (solely faith).

Ultimately Luther came to still another phrase, and this had to do with the norm or standard of truth: *sola scriptura* (solely Scripture). What good is self-denial for its own sake then? Luther felt it was worse than useless. For one thing, it had no merit whatsoever in God's sight, and it had the additional hazard of making one think that maybe his efforts pleased God – thus ALL good works had in them a real hazard — the danger of self-righteousness and Pharisaical pride!

Luther felt that it was perfectly pleasing to God for a man to be a farmer, a doctor, a businessman — and it was also wholly right to marry, own your home, and live a normal life — PROVIDED one puts his trust in God through Christ, and goes faithfully to church to hear the Word and receive the sacrament. Of course to arrive at all this understanding of the Christian life took time.

A few years after this earth-shaking tower experience Luther was deeply shocked. He discovered that the people of the Wittenberg area were flocking across the border into the territory of Albert, Margrave of Brandenburg. He was a young man in his twenties, but by a generous use of money had been able to secure the office of Archbishop of Magdeburg, 1513, and Archbishop and Elector of Mainz, 1514. But he had had to pay a pretty sum to Rome to acquire this concentration of power. He worked out a grand scheme to recoup his finances. He would *sell* indulgences, telling the people that the money would be used for the construction of the great St. Peter's Cathedral in Rome. But actually, he himself would send only half the money to Rome; the other half he would keep.

The sale of the indulgences was locally in the hands of a man named John Tetzel. A comprehensive scale of payments was worked out, charging ever higher rates for the indulgences as one went up the social scale. It was represented that one could even buy deceased loved ones out of purgatory, and that — best of all — this did not require a contrite heart on the part of the one making the gift for the redemption of the dead! All this was a grievous abuse of the power of the Keys (supposedly held by the pope), as far as Luther was concerned.

Luther, a young theologian in his thirty-fourth year, therefore addressed a gracious letter to the archbishop, a young man of twenty-seven, reporting to him the dreadful traffic in indulgences which was going on in his bishopric, and addressing him with medieval courtesy as, "Reverend Father in Christ." (It never occurred to Luther that the reverend father was behind the whole scheme, much less that he was getting half the profit!)

On this occasion, October 31, 1517, Luther enclosed a list of ninety-five statements ("theses") about indulgences for the contemplation of the archbishop. Luther begged the margrave (he was a secular ruler as well as an archbishop) to put a stop to the whole awful business, and added that if he failed to do so, Luther feared the consequences. But Albert's only concern was to stop Luther from making trouble. Albert immediately asked the faculty of the University of Mainz for their evaluation of Luther's ninety-five theses, and also sent a copy to Rome.

It seems ironical that a young monk, priest, and professor should have had the audacity to defy the whole Catholic Church of which he considered himself a faithful and obedient member. But one development led to another. The church refused to yield to Luther's scruples on indulgences, and Luther in turn became more and more excited about the authority of Holy Scripture.

At the same time Luther became less and less confident that the bishops and councils could never err — even the popes! The former timid monk was fast becoming a lionhearted reformer. The climax came in 1521 when Luther stood on trial before the Parliament ("Diet") of the empire, with the emperor of the Holy Roman Empire, Charles V, in the chair. There to accuse Luther was his Catholic opponent, Dr. John Eck, a learned theologian and a bitter enemy of the basic convictions of Luther. Eck tried to pin heresy on Luther. He demanded that Luther recant his errors. Luther asked for time. The next day he stood before the Diet and proclaimed firmly and clearly that he could not put his trust in councils and popes, for they had often erred. He continued, "My conscience is taken captive by God's Word, and I neither can nor will revoke anything. . . . God help me, Amen."

Luther had been formally excommunicated from the church early in 1521, and his friends had warned him not to go to Worms in the first place. Remember, they warned him, what happened to Hus — even though he too was given a *safe-conduct*. But Luther declared his readiness to go to the Diet even though there were "as many devils there as there are tiles on the roofs." Luther had an inner compulsion to speak up for what he considered the only infallible Guide and Rule for the church of Christ — the Word of God.

Luther had a powerful friend in the ruler of Electoral Saxony, the duke known as Frederick the Wise, a man of fifty-eight, and the founder of the University of Wittenberg. Frederick was a good solid man, and although subject to the emperor, was not minded to let that youth of twenty-one destroy such a great and good man of God as Luther. He therefore commissioned a party of horsemen to "capture" Luther on his way home from Worms and to hide him.

Frederick took care not to learn where that was, so that he could honestly tell the emperor that he simply did not know where Luther was. As "Knight George" the bearded Luther lived in the Wartburg Castle from May 1521 until the spring of 1522, during which time he continued with his studies. About Christmas time, 1521, he got the idea to translate the Greek New Testament into German, and in a few months had the first draft ready for correction and revision; it was published in September 1522, a tremendous success. (There had been fifteen printings of the German Bible between 1466 and 1522, but it was a poor translation, of uneven quality, and did not "sound German" — it read like a translation of a foreign work. Luther made Christ and the apostles "talk like Germans." Luther completed the whole Bible in 1534, and it remains a monument to the learning and linguistic skill of its translator.)

Luther finally got around in his forty-second year to getting married. In June of 1525 he was united in marriage with a former Cistercian nun, Catharine von Bora, twenty-six. Although they were both vigorous and strong-willed persons, they had a happy home **and were blessed with three sons and three** daughters. Catharine lived with Luther twenty-one years until his death in 1546. She died six years later.

In A.D. 1054 the great East-West schism occurred, with the Eastern Church going under the name of the Orthodox Church, and with the Western Church being called Roman Catholic. (The Eastern Church has no pope, has many married priests, and differs on a number of other points from the Catholic Church.)

Luther had no intention of tearing a huge chunk of the Catholic Church from Rome. Luther wrote to Archbishop Albert in 1517: "I pray that you may accept this humble but faithful admonition graciously . . . even as I submit it with a faithful and devoted heart. For I, too, am one of your sheep." As late as 1520 Luther could still address the pope with genuine courtesy, even writing, "So I come, Holy Father Leo, and lie prostrate at your feet."

But he went on to say that he could not back down from the teaching of the Word of God. The state of corruption in the Roman Church in those turbulent years, 1517-21, when the tension between Luther and Rome went on to a total break, was too great to accept correction. The consequence was that slowly and reluctantly — yet with great joy — Luther saw his supporting princes set up territorial evangelical churches, which in spite of his objections came to be known as Lutheran churches.

This process began in 1526. Melanchthon, most notable assistant to Luther, wrote, and Luther revised, a *Kirchenordnung* (a church ordinance which served as a sort of confession of faith, directory for public worship, etc.). Melanchthon also wrote a comprehensive statement of Christian doctrine, the *Augsburg Confession of Faith*, 1530. In spite of the Thirty Years War (1618-48) between Catholic and Lutheran forces, a huge part of Germany, as well as the Scandinavian lands, became and remained Lutheran.

The Lutheran Church, still a vigorous champion of "Justification by Faith," is now also strong in North America. Needless to say, Luther and his churches rejected all doctrines and practices which were part of the tradition of the Medieval Church, but contrary to the Bible: prayer to the saints, masses for the dead, purgatory, the papacy, compulsory celibacy of priests, works of merit, the doctrine of seven sacraments, etc.

Luther was a man of prayer, a devout Bible student, a competent Bible translator, a mighty preacher of God's Word, an organizer, a man of unusual courage, a prolific author, a good theologian, a hymn writer, and a family man. In controversy he often became somewhat coarse and rough, using ridicule, sarcasm, and satire. (He one time wrote to the pope: "In life I was thy pestilence; dying, I will be thy death, O Pope.") In arguing with Caspar Schwenckfeld, he called him *Stenkfeld,* that is, a stinking field. But this was a common literary style in the sixteenth century.

Zwingli, the Swiss Reformer

In Northern Switzerland, which is German-speaking to this day, the chief reformer was a gifted and learned priest named Huldrych (Ulrich in English) Zwingli. Born on New Year's Day, 1484, Zwingli was just a few months younger than Luther. His birthplace was the village of Wildhaus, located in the Toggenburg Valley of the Canton of St. Gall. His uncle, Bartholomew Zwingli, was the village priest.

Zwingli's early education was secured in Switzerland (Wesen, Basel, Bern), after which he attended the University of Vienna, 1500-2, followed by four years at the Swiss University of Basel where he earned his BA degree in 1504, and his MA in 1506. That same year he was ordained priest by the bishop of Constance and accepted his first parish, Glarus, in the canton of the same name. There he served ten years, during which time he served as a military chaplain and accompanied the troops into Italy.

In his heart, Zwingli came to the awareness that the Catholic Church needed reform. But he held his peace for a time. During this decade in Glarus he became proficient in his mastery and use of the Greek language, which he used to read the Greek classics, the church fathers, and the Greek New Testament. From 1516 to the end of 1518 Zwingli served as priest in the town of Einsiedeln in the Canton of Schwyz, a town famous for its Benedictine abbey and shrine, to which thousands of pilgrims came each year. This matter of pilgrimages also bothered the priest.

Zwingli himself claimed that he began to understand the "gospel" of God's grace in the year 1516. He also began to preach the gospel, but his transition to the new message was cautious and gentle, and was not accompanied by violent attacks on Catholic doctrines or practices. Zwingli did vigorously oppose the seller of indulgences, Bernardin Samson, in August 1518, and Zurich refused him admission. At the end of that year, Zwingli accepted the post of priest in the Great Minster (cathedral) of Zurich, where he began his ministry the first Sunday of 1519, a ministry in which he exposited entire books, section by section, with skill and exceptional success. His own moral life had never been entirely chaste, but that was a common failure in priests of that era. But now as an evangelical man, it troubled him.

Zwingli joined others in begging the bishop of Constance to allow the priests honorably to marry — or at least to wink at their marriages — but in vain. In 1519 Zwingli almost died of the plague, and in 1520 his brother did die; and both events had a sobering effect on him. In 1522 he secretly began living with a widow, Anna Reinhard Meyer, whom he publicly married on April 2, 1524. During Lent, 1522, Zwingli watched some Zurich Christians eat a bite of meat in defiance of Catholicism, and he vigorously defended them.

During 1523 and 1524 one Catholic practice after another was abolished in Zurich, by the government, to be sure, but as taught and advocated by Zwingli. Organs and works of art were removed from the church buildings; monasteries were closed down; images and relics were done away. The mass was not abolished fully until Holy Week, 1525, when Zurich observed its first evangelical Lord's Supper on April 13.

Zwingli was not an opponent of the fine arts; he himself loved and enjoyed good music, for example. But once he was an earnest "Protestant" reformer, he put the Word of God and the gospel first in the life of the church. The church building was to be a plain and

Questions for Review, Thought, and Further Reading

1. Why was Luther in severe distress prior to his tower experience?
2. Why was Luther so long blind to the doctrine of "righteousness by faith"?
3. What verse was the key that unlocked the biblical plan of salvation for Luther?
4. What were the two sources of authority for the Catholic Church? What was Luther's position on this matter?
5. Did Luther wish the evangelical church he founded to be named after him? Should it have been called Lutheran?
6. How did Zwingli's discovery of the gospel differ from Luther's?
7. Describe some major differences between Luther and Zwingli.

5

Tbe ANABaptist-Mennonite Tradition

Protestant Disunity

There were various non-Catholic religious groups at many points during the long history of the Medieval Church, as set forth by Leonard Verduin in his monograph, *The Reformers and Their Stepchildren* (Eerdmans, 1964). As we saw earlier, the ancient church divided into Orthodox (East) and Roman Catholic (West) in A.D. 1054.

In the sixteenth century, the several Protestant churches emerged from Catholicism: the Lutherans in Germany; the Reformed in Switzerland, France, and the Netherlands; the Presbyterians in Scotland (under John Knox); and the Church of England in Great Britain (where one of the chief reformers was Thomas Cranmer). John Wesley (1703-91) later set out to revive and renew the Church of

England, but out of his efforts emerged the great Methodist Church, a body separate from the church to which he tried to bring renewal. It is most unfortunate the way the Protestant rediscovery of the gospel tended to be accompanied by an individualistic spirit which made Protestant unity a non-reality.

The Swiss Brethren

One of the men who was brought to a personal conversion from sin to Christ was a young patrician in Zurich, Switzerland, Conrad Grebel (c. 1498-1526) by name. In some ways Grebel's career followed that of his mentor, Zwingli. Grebel studied at the University of Basel (1514-15), at the University of Vienna (1515-18), and at the University of Paris (1518-20): at the latter two with scholarship aid supplied by the Austrian emperor and the king of France respectively. Grebel planned to study further at the University of Pisa, with a papal grant, but ill health and a love affair which culminated in marriage prevented the Pisa sojourn.

In 1522 Grebel married his beloved Barbara, a union later graced with three children. That was also the year of Grebel's conversion, through the preaching, and the personal fellowship and friendship of the older Zwingli. For over a year Grebel was proud to stand at Zwingli's side in his great reform work, and grateful to

God for the mighty strides which Zwingli was leading the governmental authorities to take.

Tension was evident between Zwingli and Grebel by the fall of 1523, however. Somehow Grebel had begun to feel that Zwingli was too slow and lukewarm. Grebel also came to the conclusion that it was not right for Zwingli always to defer to the civil authorities on the tempo of the reformation changes. Grebel gradually developed the conviction that only the Word of God and the Spirit of God should be the guides in the work of God's people, the church.

By 1524 Grebel was holding stubbornly to what Zwingli had believed and taught earlier — even as recently as 1523 — namely, that it would be best to defer the baptism of children until they came to years of understanding, and then to give them catechetical instruction as the ancient church did in the fourth century. In September 1524, Grebel set forth his vision for the church in a long letter of two parts, addressed to Thomas Muentzer, a reformer of North Germany, two of whose tracts had found their way to Switzerland, and whom Grebel did not know. (Incidentally, the letter was never delivered, but was brought back to Switzerland, where it still is. Herald Press published this letter, both in the original German and in English translation, 1970.)

The richest delights in Grebel's life came in

the Bible study sessions in which he and his friends gathered around the Word of God and engaged in Bible study and prayer. Perhaps Grebel's closest colleague was Felix Manz.

If Grebel was disappointed in Zwingli, it could also be said that Zwingli was disappointed and hurt by what seemed like arrogance in Grebel. In December of 1524 they made an effort to get together, but could not, agree. On January 10, 1525, they had another fruitless dialogue. Finally, on Tuesday, January 17, 1525, they and their respective supporters engaged in a solemn debate before the Council of the 200 in Zurich. The 200 senators decided at the end of the day that Zwingli had shown that infant baptism was not a bad thing (*nichts unrechtes*).

On this occasion Grebel argued for a free church, not one established by law, with freedom of conscience, each person being free to accept or reject the gospel, with those who accepted sealing their vows of discipleship to Christ by water baptism. Zwingli was not minded to break the union of church and state — which went all the way back to A.D. 380, and in spirit even to the Roman Emperor Constantine the Great, who ruled A.D. 306-337. He also rejected his earlier view on the desirability of believer's baptism — much to Grebel's anguish.

Now the Council went into action. The next

day, Wednesday, January 18, 1525, they decreed that any parents delaying more than eight days in having their babies christened would be exiled from the land. Another blow fell on Saturday, January 21, when the Council issued an order for Grebel and Manz to cease convening Bibly study groups. What a blow to their spirits! What should they do? They called a meeting that Saturday night to face the issue together. The longer they talked, the more serious it looked. They finally fell on their knees and cried to God for His help and leading.

When they arose from their prayer, an amazing and unplanned scene unfolded. One of those present was a priest named George from the town of Chur in the canton known as the Grisons (Graubünden in German). He then and there declared to the natural leader of the group, Grebel, that he wished to be baptized upon his faith in Christ. Grebel complied. Thereupon the others, possibly fifteen in number, asked George to baptize them. He also complied. Thus the decree which was intended to suppress forever the sentiment for a Free Church led straight to the organization of the first modern Free Church!

Zurich reacted with vigor. Soon there were imprisonments of the *Swiss Brethren* members (as they came to be called later), both men and women. The summer of 1526 Conrad Grebel's father, Jacob Grebel, a minority leader in the Zurich senate, was beheaded, a severe sentence for the financial item held against him (accepting pensions from foreign rulers) — but this of course did away with a man who did not favor extreme measures against the Swiss Brethren of whom his son was the leader.

Even as early as May 29, 1525, however, one of the Catholic cantons, Schwyz, had burned at the stake a Swiss Brethren member, Hippolyus ("Bolt") Eberli, for this was a common way Catholic lands dealt with those they considered heretics. Zurich did not put anyone to death until January 5, 1527, when Felix Manz was drowned in the Limmat River by the authorities for having taught such principles as a free church, religious toleration, and the rejection of capital punishment and war. His body lies buried in an unmarked grave in the cemetery of the St. Jacob's Church in Zurich.

That same day the priest George from Chur (commonly known as Blaurock or Bluecoat) was beaten almost to death, but being a non-citizen of Zurich was merely banished. He was later (September 6, 1529) after torture burned at the stake in the Tirol. Meanwhile, Grebel, after being in and out of prison for his evangelistic efforts in various parts of Northern Switzerland, died of the plague the summer of 1526 at Maienfeld in the Grisons — a town in which one of his sisters lived. Those who followed Grebel were then commonly known as *Täufer* (a German word meaning Baptizers), but they simply called each other Brethren. Their opponents often called them Anabaptists (Greek for Re-baptizers), a term of reproach which lumped together people of quite varied ideas and styles of life.

Although the persecution of the Swiss Brethren was severe, with many dying as martyrs, the church had remarkable vitality and growth. By Easter, 1525, the congregation at St. Gall numbered 500. Persecution unto the death lasted almost a century, and even in the eighteenth century imprisonment and sentences of galley slavery occurred. One bishop was jailed in the nineteenth century for baptizing a person not of a Swiss Anabaptist (Mennonite) family! Emigration took a heavy toll also, so that there are today only about 2,000 Mennonites in Switzerland.

Link to the Netherlands

The second cradle of the Mennonite Church was the Netherlands. And the man who carried the ideas of a free church, of believer's baptism, and of nonresistance to the Low Countries of the North was, oddly enough, not a member of the Swiss Brethren Church but an ex-Lutheran preacher who became a sort of free-lance Anabaptist herald. His name was Melchior Hofmann (or as he wrote it, Hoffman).

Born in Swabia, Hofmann began his ministry of the Word of God in 1525. But by 1526 he was more Zwinglian and Anabaptist than Lutheran, and soon thereafter he agreed more with the Anabaptists than with the Zwinglians. In addition, however, to the major tenets of the Anabaptists he was a sort of specialist on prophecy, preaching flaming sermons on Daniel and the Book of Revelation, making prophetic predictions, and taking a great interest in dreams, visions, and special revelations from God.

Because of these emphases the Swiss Brethren could not recognize him as a brother in their fellowship, and he in turn could not recognize them, for they lacked the flair which he had for what is known as apocalyptic literature (emphasizing the visions of the Book of Revelation, e.g.).

One of his followers sent out emissaries two by two in the Netherlands to spread the message of Melchior. Two of them came to Leeuwarden in Friesland in December 1533 and baptized a man named Obbe Philips, among others. A week later another pair of evangelists baptized his brother, Dirk Philips. For almost two years the Philips brothers were ministers of a small band of peaceful (nonresistant) Melchiorites in Friesland. Unfortunately, there were other Melchiorites — they might be called Ultra-Melchiorites — who came to think it is legitimate to use force toward a good end. The spring of 1534 the differences came to a head. Obbe, Dirk, and some others tore themselves loose from the unbalanced preoccupation that Melchior had taught, purged the movement from any unbiblical elements as they understood it, and continued on with their ministry in what might be called the Obbenite Brotherhood.

The Münster Tragedy

The spring of 1534 marked a new and horrible development on the part of the more apocalyptic Melchiorites. (Hofmann was by this time sitting in prison in Strassburg where he died, after serving ten years, in 1543.) Their leader was a Dutch carnal opportunist named Jan Matthijs. He led his followers to Münster in Westphalia and succeeded in an unbelievable manner in getting the civil control of the city which he then transformed into a sort of theocracy. The Catholic bishop called out his army and laid siege to the city.

Matthijs was killed in a skirmish with the army, but was succeeded by a worse character, Jan of Leiden, who actually crowned himself king, instituted polygamy in the city, set up a communism of consumption, and rode out the siege until June 1535, when his starving and deceived subjects betrayed the city into the hands of the bishop's forces.

This tragic development may have resulted

indirectly from the preoccupation of Hofmann with the apocalyptic, but it was actually contrary to all he stood for. Much less did it represent the simple nonresistant faith of the Frisian Obbenites and of the Swiss Brethren. The Münster debacle is a nightmare in church history.

Menno

In the long run the man who did the most for the peaceful Anabaptists was a man named Menno, son of a Frisian named Simon. He is therefore known as Menno Simons, although that is an accidental name, for he might just as well have been called Menno of Witmarsum, the name of his native village. Born about 1496 Menno received training as a Roman priest, and was consecrated to that office the spring of 1524, at twenty-eight.

About a year after his ordination he was celebrating the mass, and when he said in Latin, *This is my body*, he knew that the miracle of transubstantiation occurred. But somehow the thought inexplicably came to him, Does this miracle really happen? This blasphemous thought Menno attributed to the devil, supposing that Satan was trying to seduce him away from the holy faith. Menno therefore went to the confessional with his sinful thought. Yet he could not forget it. Time after time it would haunt him.

Menno finally did that which he had never done before: he took up the New Testament. He confesses that he had not read very far until he felt that "we were deceived" — meaning he and his Catholic friends. Yet he feared to leave the Catholic Church, lest he wind up in hell. It was the writings of Luther which ultimately brought solace to Menno; Luther helped him see that the violation of human doctrines and commandments could not lead to damnation.

In 1531 Menno had a second traumatic experience. He heard of a man named Sicke being beheaded at Leeuwarden in Friesland for accepting believer's baptism. (He was variously known as Sicke Freerks — son of Frederick — or Sicke Snijder — that is, tailor. The execution took place on March 20, 1531, the first Anabaptist martyr in the Netherlands, the first of about 2,500 in the Low Countries, i.e., the Netherlands and Belgium.

This really troubled Menno. In his very heart he was convinced that the Catholic Church taught an unbiblical doctrine of communion: was it also unbiblical in baptizing babies? After much research and reading, including the New Testament, he concluded that it actually was in error on the matter! Still Menno dallied. He did not leave the church.

The spring of 1535 his own brother got caught up in a revolutionary and fanatical movement, and joined in an insurrection against the government. In the insurrection Menno's brother lost his life. It smote his conscience to think that his deluded brother was at least manly enough to die for what he thought was the truth. Whereas Menno was certain that he himself knew what the truth was, but he was unwilling to follow it.

This broke Menno's heart. He wept; he repented; he came to Christ in penitence and heartfelt faith. He felt that Christ accepted him, and gave him a new heart. After preaching another nine months in his Catholic pulpit (he served at Pingjum, 1524-31, and at nearby Witmarsum, 1531-36), he renounced Catholicism on or about Sunday, January 30, 1536, and went into hiding. God used him here and there, however, to proclaim the gospel to lost men and women, and he was able to lead some to repentance and faith.

Possibly a year after his withdrawal from Catholicism a group of peaceful Obbenites called on Menno in behalf of their brotherhood, begging him to accept the office of bishop (then also called elder). Menno declined. But the brethren persisted, and ultimately Menno yielded. Obbe reports that he ordained Menno (as bishop) in the province of Groningen. Menno served for a quarter century, first in Holland (1536-43), during which time Emperor Charles V issued a decree for Menno's arrest, and promising a handsome reward for turning him in; Menno then served in the Rhineland (1543-46), and finally in Holstein (1546-61), then a part of Denmark, but now in North Germany.

In January 1561, Menno was on his deathbed in his home at Wuestenfelde, between Hamburg and Lübeck. On the twenty-fifth anniversary of his renunciation of Catholicism he took a turn for the worse, and the next day, Friday, January 31, 1561, in his sixty-fifth year, he died. Menno's wife Gertrude, and a son Jan, had passed away before that time, but as late as 1558 he still had living daughters.

Besides giving exceptionally fine leadership to his brotherhood during his life (his followers were designated as *Mennists* as early as 1545 in East Friesland) Menno left at his death a total of twenty-five books and booklets, which with the *Martyrs Mirror* of T. J. van Braght of 1660, have exerted an enormous influence on Mennonites down through the centuries. Both the *Complete Writings* of Menno (second printing of the Verduin-Wenger edition, 1966) and the *Martyrs Mirror* are to this day enjoying a lively sale.

Anabaptist Emphases

If we were able to ask Grebel or Menno what is really central in the Christian message, they would probably say something like this:

We believe in one God: Father, Son, and Holy Spirit. We believe that Jesus Christ was God in the flesh, that He died for our sins, and that by His death He broke the enslaving power of the demonic forces of evil, and liberated us from the slavery of sin. We believe that the risen and ascended Christ sent the Holy Spirit upon His waiting people on the day of Pentecost. We believe that the Holy Spirit still accompanies the reading and proclamation of the Word of God, convicting men of sin and wooing them to repentance and faith. We believe in the separation of church and state, that the only authorities in the church are the Word of God and the Spirit of God. We believe it to be the privilege and the commission of the members of Christ's church to witness to all men that Christ died for them, and that God desires the salvation of all. Those who repent and are ready for the commitments of Christian faith and discipleship are to be baptized with water, thus sealing their vows of discipleship to Christ.

We believe that infants and children stand in no need of any ceremony, for they are by the word of Christ already in His kingdom. We believe it is the nature and the obligation of Christ's disciples to willingly take up their individual crosses — to be ready to bear, even unto death, whatever it may cost them to follow Christ faithfully. This means a readiness to accept unjust suffering in meekness and love. And it involves a renunciation of force and violence in human relations.

We believe that when one is received into the Christian church he is committing himself to give counsel and to receive counsel from the brotherhood, and that the brotherhood must accept responsibility to keep a loving eye on each member, so as to help each one, through encouragement, warning, and intercessory prayer, to live a life of holiness, love, and obedience. That is, the church is a disciplined body, not under magistrates and state officials, but under the authority of the Word and the Spirit of God.

We believe that the Christian life is one of careful obedience to the New Testament, both in its spirit and in its letter, and for this reason no oaths should be sworn. We believe that the Spirit of God seeks to bring each Christian to, and to maintain in him, a spirit of brokenness and 'penitence, ready to accept correction and instruction from the brethren, and filled with the peace and joy of the Holy Spirit.

We believe that all the blessings of the Christian life are appropriated by personal faith. We believe that the ordinances (sacraments) of the church are joyful group celebrations of the blessings of being in Christ. We believe that the style of life of Christians should be a witness, and a rebuke, to those who live in secularism, in carnality, in violence and bloodshed, in materialism, and in any other form of that revolt against God which the Bible designates as sin and disobedience.

We believe that the Christian church should, in humility and love, give a clear witness against all forms of personal sin and of social injustice. We believe that although the Christian life is a continual warfare against the demonic forces in society and in human nature, yet even in its suffering it is one of deep inner peace, and it issues in real joy.

We believe that the earmark of the Christian is caring love, both for those already in the church, and for those who have not yet found the Savior and His way of the cross. We look forward in hope to the return of our Lord Jesus Christ as Savior and Judge.

The Baptist Church

One of the largest Protestant churches in America is the Baptists, a denomination with about 30 million members around the globe in 1970. The chief founder of the Baptists in England was John Smyth, who led his tiny congregation to Holland to escape persecution, and who in 1608 baptized himself and others. The next year he applied to the Dutch Mennonites for membership, but it was not until 1615 that his followers were received into the

Mennonite Church. He himself died in 1612.

But his disciple, Thomas Helwys, had broken with Smyth on uniting with the Mennonites, and in 1611 had led his followers back to England where he formally established the General Baptist Church, which was "Arminian" (non-Calvinistic as to doctrines such as election and predestination) in character.

In many respects these London Baptists resembled the original Anabaptists, especially Balthasar Hübmaier, for they held to a free church and believer's baptism. On the other hand, they did not reject the oath, the magistracy, and participation in the military.

About 1616 a Calvinistic group of Baptists emerged in England under the leadership of a man named Henry Jacob; because of their doctrine of election they were nicknamed Particular Baptists. A group of Particular Baptists adopted immersion in 1633. The General and Particular Baptists of England merged as recently as 1891. All Baptists now baptize by immersion in water.

The founders of the American Baptist Church were Roger Williams and Ezekiel Holliman, at Providence, Rhode Island, 1639. The Rhode Island (and American) Baptists introduced baptism by immersion as the result of the influence of Mark Lukar who joined the congregation at Newport, Rhode Island, in 1644.

Baptists stress separation of church and state, believer's baptism, freedom of conscience, religious toleration, missions and evangelism, Sunday schools, and Christian education. They have done much to bring the Blacks of America to Christianity. One of their outstanding leaders, Culbert G. Rutenber, has written a vigorous defense of Christian pacifism entitled, *The Dagger and the Cross*. (Consult the article, "Baptists," in such reference works as the *Mennonite Encyclopedia*.)

Questions for Review, Thought, and Further Reading

1. Summarize the pre-conversion life of Grebel. What brought him to conversion?
2. Why did Grebel break with Zwingli? What were the issues?
3. Describe the momentous scene of Saturday night, January 21, 1525, when the first modern Free Church (Mennonite now) was born.
4. Describe the deaths of Grebel, Manz, and Blaurock.
5. Who carried Anabaptist ideas from the South to the Netherlands?
6. Contrast the Münsterites with the Obbenites.
7. Trace the course of Menno's life and service.
8. Do you agree with the Anabaptist emphases?

6

ThE MODERN MISSIONARY MOVEMENT

Catholic Missions

In the sixteenth century the Protestant state churches were remarkably indifferent to foreign mission work. In his *History of Christianity: Readings in the History of the Church from the Reformation to the Present*, Professor Clyde L. Manschreck tries to account for this phenomenon. He says that as recently as 1651 the Wittenberg Theological faculty held that the gospel had really been carried into all the world, and that the heathen must therefore be considered as being under the judgment of God.

It was Catholic missionaries who went out to various non-Christian lands with the Word of God in the days of the Reformation. A splendid example of missionary concern would be Francis Xavier (1506-52). Born of a

Basque family in Navarre, he was educated in Paris, where he remained for a time as a teacher of philosophy. In 1534 he helped found the Catholic Jesuit order. In 1537 he was ordained a priest in Venice, Italy, and in 1541 Portugal's King John III sent him to Goa, a Portuguese territory in India. He first preached in Goa and along the southwest coast of India.

In all, Xavier spent seven years in the East Indies and the Malayan Archipelago. In 1549 he went on to Japan, where he labored two more years. He then tried to organize a mission to China but died before he got there. He had good success in winning converts to Christianity in Ceylon. He always had to preach through an interpreter. Manschreck states that Xavier "exemplified the dedication and perseverance" of the Roman missionaries of the sixteenth and following centuries.

The Jesuits sent missionaries to Paraguay in South America in 1586 where they taught the Guarani Indians Christianity, agriculture, and even some manufacturing, and established a Jesuit government which stood almost two centuries. (In 1768 the Jesuits were expelled from Spanish America, and soon the entire Christian project in Paraguay came to nought. But it was a noble effort.)

In 1622 Rome set up the *Sacred Congregation for the Propagation of the Faith* (this in

as it now is. Perhaps it will yet be possible to approach the early church in effectiveness of local witness and outreach!

Mennonite Missions

The Anabaptists were the most missionary of all the Protestant churches in the first generation. Indeed, only the Anabaptists and the Catholics actually believed in mission work at that period of church history. Thirty-eight Anabaptist congregations were established in the canton of Zurich between 1525 and 1527, and a similar number in the canton of Bern. The so-called *Martyrs' Synod*, held at Augsburg, in August 1527, was attended by over sixty Anabaptist leaders from Switzerland, South Germany, and Austria. (See article in the *Mennonite Encyclopedia*, III, 529-31.)

Part of the concern of the conference was to enhance the unity of the Brethren; the other major concern was the evangelization of Europe. It was decided to send Hans Beck, Hans Denk, and Gregor Maler to Basel and Zurich; Peter Scheppach and Ulrich Trechsel to Worms and the Palatinate; Leonhard Dorfbrunner, Hans Mittermaier, and Leonhard Schiemer to Upper (Southern) Austria; George Nespitzer to Franconia; Eucharius Binder and Joachim Maerz to Salzburg; and Leonard Pruckh and Leonhard Spoerle to Bavaria. This list is probably far from complete.

We know of the synod only through the testimonies of those put to death. Binder and Maerz died at the stake at Salzburg, October 27, 1527; Spoerle was executed November 12, 1527; Hut died of a fire which broke out in his prison cell at Augsburg, December 6, 1527; Dorfbrunner was burned at the stake at Passau, in January 1528; Schiemer was beheaded at Rattenberg, January 14, 1528; etc. Many others of the participants were executed, usually after severe torture.

Church and state joined hands to destroy the Free Churchmen who dared to teach separation of church and state, believer's baptism, and the way of the cross in unjust suffering (nonresistance). The day of religious toleration had not yet dawned. (It should be added that a few of the early missioners, broken in body and spirit, recanted their Anabaptist faith.) The commissioning service for the missionaries seems to have been held at Augsburg on August 24, 1527, in the home of an Anabaptist named Matthias Finder, a butcher.

Franklin H. Littell, an authority on Anabaptism, analyzes the Anabaptist theology and strategy of missions as follows: (1) The Anabaptists rejected the territorial church system and felt they were entitled to witness to all men everywhere, and those who voluntarily accepted the gospel they baptized and received into fellowship. (2) They interpreted the missionary commission of Christ to be binding on all believers at all times. (3) The lay believer was the key in the rapid spread of Anabaptism. (4) The Anabaptists regarded the suffering of the martyr church as its authentication.

Unfortunately, the persecution of the Swiss, German, Austrian, and Dutch Anabaptists was so severe for the first several generations (there were 5,000 martyrs) that the best leadership was lost, and instead of going out actively into the society in which they lived, Mennonites began to withdraw into quiet retreats of their own, having as little to do with a hostile world as possible. It appeared to them that the world simply did not want their radical type of discipleship.

As the centuries rolled on, Mennonite industry and conscientious effort to eke out a living where few people cared to live — such as the marshy deltas of the Vistula — led to some measure of financial success, so that various rulers actually welcomed these industrious farmers, who were by then content not to proselytize the members of other churches, no matter how slight their faith in and commitment to Christ. Mennonites had become the Quiet People of the land.

The first country where the missionary light began to be rekindled was the Netherlands.

An English Baptist, William H. Angas, organized in Holland, largely of Mennonites, an Aid Society to support mission work in India, 1821. Three years later a special conference of Mennonites was held in the Palatinate, and it was decided to put a box for missionary offerings in each meetinghouse.

In 1830 the Heubuden congregation, of Dutch ethnic origin, in West Prussia, held its first missionary conference. In 1847 the Mennonites of Holland organized a Dutch Mennonite Missionary Association; the president of the Association was Professor Samuel Muller of the Amsterdam Mennonite Seminary. In 1851 the first modern Mennonite missionary, Pieter Jansz of Holland, was sent to Java. Meanwhile, as early as 1827, some of the Mennonites of Russia (also of Dutch ethnic origin) had begun to support Moravian missionary projects. The first Russian Mennonite foreign missionary was Abraham Friesen of the Mennonite Brethren Conference; he went to **South India in 1889**.

The first American Mennonite mission support seems to have arisen in what is now the General Conference Mennonite Church, some of whose churches held a conference in 1855 and recognized "the high duty to support missions." From its very beginning the General Conference Mennonite Church (1860-) supported both home and foreign missionary work. Their first missionary was Samuel S. Haury, sent to the Indians of Oklahoma in 1880. Later Mennonite missions were established among the Arapahoe, Hopi, and Cheyenne Indians in Oklahoma, Arizona, and Montana.

The best linguist of the Mennonite missionaries was a Mennonite from Switzerland, Rodolphe Petter, who served with the Cheyennes from 1890. The first foreign missionary of what is now the Missionary Church (then Mennonite Brethren in Christ) was Eusebius Hershey who in 1890, at sixty-seven, went to Africa and served six months before he died.

The group known as the "Mennonite Church" (sometimes called Old Mennonites) started to hold vigorous evangelistic meetings in the 1880's, the most prominent evangelist being John S. Coffman of Elkhart, Indiana, but originally from the Shenandoah Valley of Virginia. Coffman was brought to Elkhart by the Mennonite leader, John F. Funk, the most formative figure in his denomination in recent centuries. (Funk started Mennonite publication work, 1864; initiated the formation of the Mennonite Evangelizing Committee, 1882; promoted Sunday schools from the 1860's; helped the Mennonite immigrants from Russia in the 1870's; and took the first steps in the formation of Mennonite General Conference in the 1890's).

In March 1893, Funk ordained M. S. Steiner

at the Prairie Street Mennonite Church in
Elkhart, and later that year Steiner founded
the Mennonite Mission in Chicago. The
Welsh Mountain Industrial Mission was created
by Mennonites of the Lancaster Conference
in 1898 to provide gospel privileges and em-
ployment opportunities for the Negroes of the
Welsh Mountain in Lancaster County. There was
a store, school, farm operation, shirt and broom
factories, and carpet-weaving. In 1899 Funk
commissioned the first missionaries to India:
J. A. Ressler, and W. B. Page and wife (he
was a physician).

Overseas Missions

Prior to 1900 the Old Mennonites had one
overseas mission: India. From 1900 to 1920
they established a second, in Argentina. From
1920 to 1940 they founded a third, Tanganyika
(now Tanzania). From 1940 to 1960 they entered the following countries with their
gospel witness:

Bihar, India	1940
Argentine Chaco	1943
Puerto Rico	1945
Ethiopia	1948
Sicily, Japan	1949
Belgium, Honduras	1950
England	1952
Somalia, France, Israel	1953

Nepal, Uruguay, Brazil,	
and Cuba	1954
Jamaica	1955
Ghana	1956
Vietnam	1957
Nigeria, Mexico	1958

Mennonites of the Third World

The Reformation was a European movement, and Mennonitism was its "left-wing" (less conservative, following the Scriptures more thoroughly, they believed, than did the state churches: Lutheran, Reformed, and Anglican). And so the Mennonite Church was established in the sixteenth century in Switzerland, the Netherlands, Germany, and Austria.

The second world to be penetrated by the Mennonites was North America, wholly by immigration at first. In modern times, largely since 1850, the Mennonites of Europe and of North America have entered the so-called "Third World" with the gospel of Christ. This world includes the American Indians, the Negroes of North America and of Africa, the great nations of China and Japan, the Spanish of North and South America, and the vast millions of Indonesia. God has richly blessed this mission outreach, so that by 1970 there were members of the Mennonite World Conference in many lands, some of the main bodies having approximately the following numbers of baptized members:

Congo	45,000	Nigeria	5,000
India	30,000	China	4,000
Indonesia	30,000	Japan	1,500
Tanzania	8,000	Ethiopia	600

Every continent has Mennonites living on it, including a hundred in Australia. (For a full list of the Mennonites in the various countries of the world, see the statistics in the annual *Mennonite Yearbook*, Scottdale, Pa.)

God be praised for the way He has blessed this endeavor to make disciples of all the nations (Matthew 28:18-20)!

Home Missions

Space does not allow a survey of the vast number of mission outposts and full mission churches established by the Old Mennonites, for the most part since 1900, and especially since 1935. Let us take just one district conference, Franconia in Southeastern Pennsylvania. As an example:

From 1700 to 1800 the following permanent congregations were established:

Skippack	Salford
Methacton	Line Lexington
Providence	Franconia
Hereford	Rockhill

Boyertown
Swamp
Plains
Towamencin

Doylestown
Blooming Glen
Deep Run
Vincent

From 1800 to 1900 the following were added:
Souderton   Hersteins   Groveland   (Bertolets)

From 1900 to 1930 the following mission
outposts/churches:
Perkasie   Norristown   Pottstown

From 1930 to 1960:

Finland
Spring Mount
Perkiomenville
Lansdale
Morris
Ambler
Centereach
Estella
Bartonsville
Bristol
Trevose
Rocky Ridge

Easton
Lambertville
Levittown
Bethany
Taftsville
Bridgeport
Conshohocken
Haycock
Salem
Allentown
Steel City
Gelatt

This is none other than the hand of Christ.
It is possible for a church which may have
lost its basic commission to be aroused from
its lethargy and to experience renewal as it
awakens to the needs of men — spiritual and
material — beginning at "Jerusalem" and

moving out to all of "Judea," and going on to "Samaria," and literally "to the ends of the earth." God raised up men like John F. Funk and John S. Coffman to bring a spiritual revival to the Mennonite brotherhood, and the story is being repeated decade after decade by local men and women who have to some extent at least recaptured the missionary motif of the original Anabaptists — as Mennonites were known four centuries ago.

Explanatory Note: There are two main cradles of the Mennonites of North America: (1) Switzerland, where Conrad Grebel founded the church in 1525, and (2) Holland, where Obbe Philips broke with certain unwholesome emphases of the Melchiorites in 1534, and where Menno Simons served the brotherhood so effectively. Three permanent denominations came out of these two movements: (1) the Mennonites, (2) the Hutterites, and (3) the Amish. The three largest bodies of Mennonites are (1) the Old Mennonites, officially simply the Mennonite Church, with over 100,000 members, including mission fields; (2) the Mennonite Brethren, with 65,000, including mission fields, and (3) the General Conference Mennonites, with 54,000 members in North America — not counting the mission fields where they are in some cases in cooperation with other Mennonite groups; in the Congo, for example, there are about 45,000 members, and the work is a joint effort of the General Conference Mennonites with some of the smaller conferences of Mennonites.

Questions for Review, Thought, and Further Reading

1. Describe early Catholic missionary efforts in the sixteenth century.
2. Who was John Eliot, and what did he do for the outreach of Christ's church?
3. Describe the contribution of William Carey: in Christendom, and in India.
4. Describe the gradual growth of conviction for missions in Protestantism.
5. When, where, and how did the Mennonites begin again to become missionary and evangelistic, as the Anabaptists had been?
6. Describe the work of the Welsh Mountain Industrial Mission as established in 1898.
7. In what areas do you think Christ would have the church become more active at this point in history?

7

THE CALLING OF THE CHURCH

"Ye Shall Be My Witnesses"

God's nature is such that He loves His creatures with a great and inexplicable love. He wants a people for Himself. Thus, apart from any merit in Abraham, God chose his family through his son Isaac, and the next generation He chose Jacob and his twelve sons to be the heads of the twelve tribes of Israel: His very own people.

This doctrine of God in His sovereign love is really the theme of the Bible. From the very beginning God had in mind that Israel was to serve as His witnesses to the world, showing mankind that idolatry and polytheism are dreadful errors. *Jahweh* or *Yahweh* was Israel's Hebrew name for their covenant God, and He alone is God. Israel was to be faithful to her covenant God, was to render absolute love and devotion to Him, live a life of holy obedience to His gracious instruction ("law"), and show the rest of the human race how human life can be a bit of heaven if lived in His will.

Israel was "born" as a nation at the exodus, that divine act when God by His mighty arm delivered His slave people from their bondage in the land of Egypt, brought them across the Red Sea by a show of His mercy and providential grace, and settled them as His free people in a land "flowing with milk and honey."

On the way from Egypt to Canaan God made a gracious covenant with Israel, constituting them as His sons and daughters, and giving them the right to call Him their God. He gave them His holy law, made provision for them as sinful sons of Adam by giving them a sanctuary, sacrifices for sin, and a separated priesthood to minister "in things pertaining to God." He charged them strictly to bear in mind that He did not choose them because of any inherent superiority on their part, but alone by His gracious election in love.

To further meet their needs God sent prophets to them with His holy Word, men who proclaimed His will to them, protesting against their sin, and calling them back to their law and to the God who had given them both their law and their covenant status.

Even a cursory reading of the Old Testament makes clear that Israel failed badly. She was all through her preexilic history hankering after a more sensuous form of worship, with gods that could be seen, and forms of worship which would resemble the carnality which the heathen nations around her employed in their worship. God punished His people with wars, with famines, and with pestilences (epidemics of illness): but all in vain.

Finally, He allowed the ten northern tribes to be carried off as a displaced people by the mighty nation Assyria, never to return to Israel *en masse*. Instead of taking warning from this catastrophe, the Southern Kingdom of Judah went down the same road of idolatry and immorality and social injustice as had been the ruin of the Northern Kingdom of Israel. The result was the same.

God severely chastened Judah by allowing her to be dragged off to Babylonia for seventy years of exile: and there Judah found no possibility of worshiping her covenant God on His "holy mountain," Moriah, in the beautiful temple which Solomon had built to replace the earlier tabernacle, the movable sanctuary. The Jews improvised a substitute for the temple, so that they could at least gather together to hear the law and the prophets read and explained (many of Israel's prophets had written books of their messages). This substitute was the local *synagogues* of the Jews.

What a great day it was when the Lord regathered His people, actually more from Judah than from Israel, yet a representative remnant from all twelve tribes, back in their own land and around their rebuilt temple on Mount Moriah. Once more the daily sacrifices for sin were offered up. And best of all, Israel was cured forever of her idolatrous tendencies. She was not cured of her tendency to confuse holiness with legalism, and Jewish moralistic hairsplitting covered over God's law until it was hardly recognizable.

But even then, in spite of her unworthiness, God was still able to use His failing people for His glory. A considerable number of Gentiles across the Graeco-Roman world, were so attracted to the God of Israel that they began to worship Him each Sabbath in the local synagogues of the Jews. These people were called the "Proselytes of the Gate."

In the Book of Acts they are spoken of by two Greek words which might be translated the *devout* proselytes, and the *God-fearers*. These Gentiles, along with such Jews as also repented at the preaching of Paul and other Christian leaders, formed the nucleus in each community for the chain of congregations which Paul and his co-workers established across the empire in the 40's and 50's of the first century of this era.

The Christian church was therefore nurtured in Judaism initially. God had a faithful remnant in Israel, His ancient covenant people, who followed His leading and entered the new phase of His redemptive work in the world, that is, the New Israel of God, the church. It is not the case that the Jews used to be the people of God, and now it is the church. It is rather that God always had His believing remnant, from Abraham to Christ, and through the incarnation, public ministry, atoning death, and justifying resurrection of Jesus Christ, God now brought His covenant people into a new era of blessing and privilege.

Those who by faith are "in Christ" — regardless of ethnic origin — constitute the New Humanity, the New Israel of God. And as time went on, more and more people "from every tribe and tongue and people and nation" flocked into God's New People. And this was according to the plan of God — except for the disappointing numbers of Jews who failed to see the hand of God in the establishment of His New People, and who therefore failed to claim the blessings which God willed for them all to enjoy.

The first aspect then of God's people serving as His witnessing people is for them to be a happy and free brotherhood of forgiven and forgiving people, rejoicing in the "clean slate" which God gave them in Christ.

They have a special place for each other in their hearts. In God's "congregation" (*church* in the English Bible) a great "leveling" is to take place, so that the factors which in the unredeemed society break men into classes are all wiped out.

Rich and poor, young and old, cultured and uneducated, people from every race and nation: all are to be one joyous people of God. National boundaries mean nothing, for all must be born into the kingdom of God. God's people are made "color-blind" by the love He pours into their hearts by His Spirit. These people are actually renewed. The avaricious become generous; the dishonest become honorable; the carnal become pure; the hateful become loving. This is not oratory; it is a sober description of the will of God, a will of God which is in Christ realizable, and which actually is realized insofar as people are soundly converted to the mind of Christ through their response of surrender to the Word of God and the Spirit of God.

This is the kind of church which enjoys evangelistic and missionary success. It is undoubtedly true that God sometimes — perhaps in an absolute sense, always — uses unworthy witnesses. Yet it is His will that His children "co-die" with Christ (to sin), "co-rise" with Christ (to newness of life), "co-ascend" with Christ (into the presence of God), and even "co-reign" with Christ (by a life of victory in the kingdom of God). This theme of the union of Christian believers with Christ is a common theme in the New Testament. Ephesians sets it forth with special clarity.

Such people have entered an experience of a peace "that passeth all understanding" so that they do not live from one anxiety to another, depending on world news or local trials and tribulations. They are not tied to this world, but regard the experience commonly called "death" as a transition to that realm where they are "with Christ, which is far, far better," paraphrasing Paul in Philippians 1:23. God pours His love into their hearts in such measure that they are able to forgive those who sin against them. They find hatred and revenge not consonant with the new spirit which God put into them when they made their surrender to Christ as Savior and Lord. Unconverted people find them "impossible." Conversations like this are then apt to take place.

Phil: "Charlie, I have known you for some time. You don't seem to have any vices! What do you do for fun?"

Charlie (chuckling): "You have me all wrong, Phil. I have ten times as much 'fun' as I did before I was a Christian."

Phil: "You don't say so! What do you do for a good time? I don't see you drinking, dancing, reading the current novels. . . . I just don't get it."

Charlie (laughing): "You surely don't want me to preach you a sermon, do you?"

Phil: "Charlie, I'm serious. You don't go out for all the 'good times' I do, and yet you seem so happy."

Charlie: "Phil, I'll level with you. There was a time when I was miserable, trying to find genuine satisfaction in what many people call 'fun' and a 'good time.' Then I got to know a guy who didn't do the things I was doing — and not getting real joy from — and yet he seemed to have an inner peace which I lacked. So I asked him about it, and he invited me to go along to the services of his church. . . . But maybe you don't want to hear the rest of it?"

Phil: "Yes, Charlie, I do."

Charlie (earnestly): "I'll have to tell you what happened to me. I couldn't help seeing how happy this guy seemed to be among the men in his church group. They were such wholesome fellows, and they gave me a hearty welcome into their circle. I didn't feel at all like I belonged. I noticed that truck drivers, doctors, factory workers, the whole bunch of them, seemed to be genuinely happy. And any of them seemed to feel free to lead out in prayer. It just sounded like they knew the One they were talking with. Boy, did I hope they wouldn't call on me to pray! (Well, they knew better than to do that to a guy like me.)

"And then the preacher fascinated me. He seemed like such a real guy. He liked to play tennis, to go on canoe trips, and everything else. Yet it seemed that some tremendous dream had caught hold of him, and he was engaged in some sort of super project which made a center for his whole life, and gave meaning to it all. I listened to him with increasing interest and respect, and finally I had a friend buy a Bible for me. (I was too timid to do it myself.) And I began to read. My friend suggested that I read Luke, then John, then 1 Peter. The longer I read, and the more I went with my friend to church, the more I felt that there was a whole world I didn't know anything about . . . . (But maybe I am boring you.)"

Phil: "No, you're not. I want to hear the rest of it."

Charlie: "Well, I must confess that I did go through a miserable time, for a period. I began to feel that I was a guilty sinner before God, and that I needed to do something about it. I just had to do something, but I didn't know what. So I went to my friend, and told him just how miserable I was getting to feel. He put his hand on my shoulder and said, 'Charlie, the Holy Spirit is trying to get you to turn away from sin, and to become a Christian.' Well, I struggled with that for a while, and finally I told him, 'I am ready to pay any price to get right with God.' 'The only price,' he told me, 'is to break with sin, and to yield yourself to Christ.'

"Of course, I did not know how to do it; so he explained to me what Christians call 'the plan of salvation.' It wasn't complicated at all. But I must confess it made me struggle. Anyhow, I did decide to become a Christian. The man prayed with me and helped get me started. And believe me, I really am a new man. . . ."

The above description has 101 forms. Sometimes the Christian takes the initiative. Sometimes the non-Christian introduces the subject. But ordinarily the non-Christian has first of all, somehow been exposed to the Word of God in some form: memories of a childhood in a Christian home, attendance at a vacation Bible school, a tract, a radio program — the "how" varies enormously. And secondly, the non-Christian has usually been close enough to a real Christian or Christians to have sensed the reality of the Christian life. . . .

Ministering to Christ

In Matthew 25 the Lord described the judgment He will hold on the Last Day. He there made clear that we minister to Him as we minister to our fellowmen who are in need. So

Christians rejoice greatly when a "Phil" finds his way into the kingdom. But they do not stop there. Men of wealth organize to provide better housing for the poor. Christian young people volunteer to tutor underprivileged children through high school. Young people serve in general and mental hospitals for a period of "Voluntary Service" (without regular wages). Thoughtful Christians write letters to their congressmen and senators, pointing out the need for laws to be enacted which would make for greater social justice.

To be a Christian means to be *committed* — committed to do all in one's power to make it possible for all men to be persons in the full sense of the word. It is a grievous sin in God's sight for people to enslave themselves in drink or in drug addiction. And it is an even more grievous sin for men of wealth to enslave others by making it impossible for others to rise to a decent standard of living.

A real Christian simply cannot afford to live selfishly. The love of Christ will move him to do what he can in Christian compassion and caring love to lift his human brother and sister up to the possibility of a happy life — and he will use methods consistent with one who is in Christ and who cannot therefore be vengeful or hateful. Christians are interested in the *total man* and all his needs: his need for love, for understanding, for acceptance, for food, for clothing, for housing, and for salvation.

It is a poor theology which sets up a chasm between the ministry of the Word and the ministry to other human needs. Sir William Booth and thousands of other Christian leaders have shown the people of God that it is the will of Christ to minister to *all* human needs, and to do it *in the name of Christ.*

Let us get on with the task!

Questions for Review, Thought, and Further Reading

1. What moved God to choose a people for Himself?
2. What merit, if any, did God see in Israel?
3. What was Israel's responsibility to the rest of mankind?
4. How did synagogues come to be founded?
5. What were Proselytes of the Gate? What role did they play in Paul's day?
6. How many classes ought there be in the church, and how can we identify with the right one? — if this question is proper.
7. What was it that got you started on the road to Christ and His church?

8. Do you enjoy telling others of what Christ has done for you?

9. How can so many Christians seem to live for self and self-advancement, socially, financially, or otherwise — and to ignore the needy of the world?

10. Is it wrong to do "social work"? If so, why? If not, why not?

ADDITIONAL READING

In the hope that some readers may wish to do serious reading in church history, here are a few of the more accessible and valuable works in the field:

BOOKS OF SOURCES:

Joseph Cullen Ayer, Jr. *A Source Book for Ancient Church History.* Scribners, 1933

A History of Christianity:

Ray C. Petry. *Readings in the History of the Early and Medieval Church.* Prentice-Hall, 1962

Clyde L. Manschreck. *Readings . . . from the Reformation to the Present.* Prentice-Hall, 1964

American Christianity: An Historical Interpretation with Representative Documents by H. Shelton Smith, Robert T. Handy, Lefferts A. Loetscher. Vol. I, 1607-1820; Vol. II, 1820-1960. Scribners, 1960, 1963

GENERAL CHURCH HISTORY:

Roland H. Bainton. *The Church of Our Fathers.* Scribners, 1941

Karl Heussi. *Kompendium der Kirchengeschichte.* Zwoelfte, neu bearbeitete Auflage. J. C. B. Mohr (Paul Siebeck), 1960

Kenneth Scott Latourette. *A History of Christianity.* Harper & Brothers, 1953

Williston Walker. *A History of the Christian Church.* Revised by Cyril C. Richardson, Wilhelm Pauck, Robert T. Handy. Scribners, 1959

CANADIAN CHURCH HISTORY:

John Webster Grant. *The Churches and the Canadian Experience.* Ryerson Press, Toronto, 1963

H. H. Walsh. *The Christian Church in Canada.* Ryerson Press, Toronto, 1956

GROWTH OF THE CHRISTIAN CHURCH:

Kenneth Scott Latourette. *A History of the Expansion of Christianity:*

I. *The First Five Centuries*
II. *The Thousand Years of Uncertainty*
III. *Three Centuries of Advance*
IV. *The Great Century in Europe and U.S.A., 1800-1914*
V. *The Great Century in the Americas, Austral-Asia, & Africa, 1800-1914*
VI. *The Great Century in Northern Africa and Asia, 1800-1914*
VII. *Advance Through Storm, A.D. 1914 and After, with Concluding Generalizations.* Harper & Brothers, 1937-45

ANABAPTIST-MENNONITE HISTORY:

Cornelius J. Dyck, Editor. *An Introduction to Mennonite History.* Herald Press, Scottdale, Pa., Second Printing, 1967

John Horsch. *Mennonites in Europe.* Mennonite Publishing House, Scottdale, Pa., 1950

John L. Ruth, *Conrad Grebel, Son of Zurich,* Herald Press, 1975.

J. C. Wenger. *Conrad Grebel's Programmatic Letters of 1524.* Herald Press, 1970

—————. *The Mennonite Church in America.* Herald Press, 1966

The Author

J. C. Wenger, a native of Honey Brook Township, Chester County, Pennsylvania, is Professor of Historical Theology in the Associated Mennonite Biblical Seminaries, Elkhart, Indiana, a Mennonite institution. For decades he has devoted himself to the genesis and development of the Anabaptist-Mennonite tradition. He served as editor of the book, *They Met God,* and of *The Complete Writings of Menno Simons,* and is the author of *Even unto Death: The Heroic Witness of the Sixteenth-Century Anabaptists,* the *History of the Mennonites of the Franconia Conference, The Mennonites in Indiana and Michigan, Glimpses of Mennonite History and Doctrine, The Mennonite Church in America, The Doctrines of the Mennonites, Introduction to Theology, Sepa-*

rated unto God, God's Word Written, and *Conrad Grebel's Programmatic Letters of 1524.*

He has also served the Mennonites as a deacon, minister, and bishop, and as Vice President for North America of the Mennonite World Conference. He received the BA degree from Goshen College, the MA in Philosophy from the University of Michigan, and the Doctorate in Theology from the University of Zürich. He also studied at the University of Basel, the University of Chicago, and at Westminster Theological Seminary, and was a postdoctoral Visiting Fellow at Princeton Theological Seminary.

His wife is the former Ruth D. Detweiler, RN, and they are the parents of two sons and two daughters.